WORKBOOK
The Obstacle is the Way

By Ryan Holiday

PithBooks

Copyright © All Rights Reserved

Before reproducing, transmitting or photocopying any part of this book in any form or through any medium, make sure you have the necessary permissions from the author or publisher.

INTRODUCTION

Obstacles come in diverse forms. They mostly bring with them frustration, confusion, fear, anger, depression. These cripple us and prevent us from breaking out into what we may wish to achieve, or where we may want to be. Then we begin to play the blame game. We blame the system, economy, our superiors. We label our goals impossible and give up, when in reality, our attitude and approach should be our major concern.

But not everyone is incapacitated by the thought of failure. In the face of challenges, some find the strength to catapult themselves to greater grounds of success. What is different? A method and structure for comprehending and dealing with hurdles. Earlier generations braved storms and built timeless posterities because they understood this structure. They transformed weakness into strength.

We could write the similar stories for ourselves if only we try. We could turn situations around, find some benefit and use our obstacles as fuel to be where we ought to be. The process involves – perception, action and will.

PART I

PERCEPTION

ONE
THE DISCIPLINE OF PERCEPTION

Exercise

Describe one time when you had to deal with financial crisis.

_____
_____
_____
_____
_____
_____

Has there been a time when you have expressed self-discipline and objectivity in spite of agitations?

_____
_____
_____
_____
_____
_____

Recount a time in your life when you can point to as a turning point towards discipline?

_____
_____
_____
_____
_____
_____
_____
_____
_____

List five things to keep in mind when faced with obstacles?

_____
_____
_____
_____
_____
_____
_____
_____
_____

Personal Reflection

_____
_____
_____
_____
_____
_____

Goals & Objectives

_____
_____
_____
_____

Action Plan

_____
_____
_____
_____

TWO
RECOGNIZE YOUR POWER

Exercise

How do you handle unfavorable conditions?

_____
_____
_____
_____
_____
_____

Narrate an experience when it was obvious that a seemingly unpleasant situation had potential benefits.

_____
_____
_____
_____
_____
_____

Would you demonstrate your power if wrongfully accused?

_____
_____
_____
_____
_____
_____
_____
_____

Do you see mistakes as trainings?

_____
_____
_____
_____
_____
_____
_____
_____

Personal Reflection

_____
_____
_____
_____
_____
_____
_____
_____

Goals & Objectives

_____
_____
_____
_____

Action Plan

_____
_____
_____
_____
_____

THREE
STEADY YOUR NERVES

Exercise

Do you get shaken up when you run into unexpected problems?

_____
_____
_____
_____

How do you act around bullies?

_____
_____
_____
_____

List two attributes that precede skills.

_____
_____
_____
_____
_____
_____
_____

How do you prepare for sudden shock?

_____
_____
_____
_____
_____
_____
_____
_____
_____
_____
_____

Personal Reflection

_____
_____
_____
_____
_____
_____
_____

Goals & Objectives

_____
_____
_____
_____

Action Plan

_____
_____
_____
_____
_____

FOUR
CONTROL YOUR EMOTIONS

Exercise

Do you make mistakes when you panic?

_____
_____
_____
_____
_____
_____
_____
_____

How is training authority?

_____
_____
_____
_____
_____
_____

How do you keep your emotions in check?

_____
_____
_____
_____
_____
_____
_____
_____

What is apatheia?

_____
_____
_____
_____
_____
_____
_____
_____

Personal Reflection

_____
_____
_____
_____
_____
_____
_____

Goals & Objectives

_____
_____
_____
_____

Action Plan

_____
_____
_____
_____
_____

FIVE
PRACTICE OBJECTIVITY

Exercise

What is the difference between the observing eye and the perceiving eye?

_____
_____
_____
_____
_____
_____

Do you act on impulse?

_____
_____
_____
_____
_____
_____

What makes for your having clear solutions to the problems of others and not being able to figure things out when you have similar issues?

_____
_____
_____
_____
_____
_____
_____
_____

How did you solve a pressing problem?

_____
_____
_____
_____
_____
_____
_____
_____

Personal Reflection

_____
_____
_____
_____
_____
_____
_____

Goals & Objectives

_____
_____
_____
_____

Action Plan

_____
_____
_____
_____
_____

SIX
ALTER YOUR PERSPECTIVE

Exercise

Has a shift in perspective ever done you good? How?

_____
_____
_____
_____
_____
_____

How often do you consider the big picture when making decisions?

_____
_____
_____
_____
_____
_____

What are the two definitions of perspective?

_____
_____
_____
_____
_____
_____
_____
_____

In what ways do you see yourself as a solution in your career?

_____
_____
_____
_____
_____
_____
_____
_____

Personal Reflection

_____
_____
_____
_____
_____
_____
_____

Goals & Objectives

_____
_____
_____
_____

Action Plan

_____
_____
_____
_____
_____

SEVEN
IS IT UP TO YOU?

Exercise

What cause would you give your effort and energy to?

_____
_____
_____
_____
_____
_____
_____
_____

In what ways do you show an enduring spirit?

_____
_____
_____
_____

List five attributes that is up to us.

_____
_____
_____
_____
_____
_____
_____
_____
_____
_____

Name four things that are not up to us.

_____
_____
_____
_____
_____
_____
_____
_____
_____

Personal Reflection

_____
_____
_____
_____
_____
_____
_____

Goals & Objectives

_____
_____
_____
_____

Action Plan

_____
_____
_____
_____

EIGHT
LIVE IN THE PRESENT MOMENT

Exercise

List six businesses started during economic crises.

_____
_____
_____
_____
_____
_____
_____

How focused are you on the present?

_____
_____
_____
_____
_____
_____
_____

What are five things that can help you focus on the present?

_____
_____
_____
_____
_____
_____
_____

How hard are you willing to work to live in the present?

_____
_____
_____
_____
_____
_____
_____
_____

Personal Reflection

_____
_____
_____
_____
_____
_____
_____

Goals & Objectives

_____
_____
_____
_____

Action Plan

_____
_____
_____
_____
_____

NINE
THINK DIFFERENTLY

Exercise

Name three feasible things you felt were impossible while growing up.

_____
_____
_____
_____
_____

Are you open-minded?

_____
_____
_____
_____
_____
_____

How do you deal with an impossible deadline?

_____
_____
_____
_____
_____
_____
_____
_____

In your words, who is an entrepreneur?

_____
_____
_____
_____
_____
_____
_____
_____

Personal Reflection

_____
_____
_____
_____
_____
_____
_____

Goals & Objectives

_____
_____
_____
_____

Action Plan

_____
_____
_____
_____
_____

TEN
FINDING THE OPPORTUNITY

Exercise

Give reasons why you think it is possible to find opportunity in the midst of strong opposition, if you do.

_____
_____
_____
_____
_____
_____

How are your preconceptions a problem when it comes to dealing with obstacles?

_____
_____
_____
_____
_____
_____

What are five advantages of working under a bad boss?

___

Do you agree that blessings and burdens are not mutually exclusive? Give reasons.

___

Personal Reflection

_____
_____
_____
_____
_____
_____
_____

Goals & Objectives

_____
_____
_____
_____

Action Plan

_____
_____
_____
_____
_____

ELEVEN
PREPARE TO ACT

Exercise

List three attributes of proper perception.

_____
_____
_____
_____
_____
_____
_____

Do you keep a cool head when faced with problems?

_____
_____
_____
_____
_____
_____
_____

Do you face your obstacles with boldness?

_____
_____
_____
_____
_____
_____
_____
_____
_____
_____

Are you ready to take action against your obstacles?

_____
_____
_____
_____
_____
_____
_____
_____

Personal Reflection

_____
_____
_____
_____
_____
_____
_____

Goals & Objectives

_____
_____
_____
_____

Action Plan

_____
_____
_____
_____
_____

PART II

PREFACE

TWELVE
THE DISCIPLINE OF ACTION

Exercise

Narrate an instance when you were disadvantaged but did not give up.

_____
_____
_____
_____
_____

Do you make excuses for your drawbacks or do you work on yourself to get better?

_____
_____
_____
_____
_____

Explain in what ways action pays.

_____
_____
_____
_____
_____
_____
_____

List five virtues you can greet your obstacle with.

_____
_____
_____
_____
_____
_____
_____
_____
_____
_____
_____

Personal Reflection

_____
_____
_____
_____
_____
_____
_____

Goals & Objectives

_____
_____
_____
_____

Action Plan

_____
_____
_____
_____
_____

THIRTEEN
GET MOVING

Exercise

To what extent will you go to achieve your dreams, when the conditions are not perfect?

_____
_____
_____
_____
_____
_____

How often do you keep going, even after your first achievement?

_____
_____
_____
_____
_____

Do you take risks?

_____
_____
_____
_____
_____
_____
_____
_____

Name three places where Rommel won victory?

_____
_____
_____
_____
_____
_____
_____
_____
_____

Personal Reflection

_____
_____
_____
_____
_____
_____
_____

Goals & Objectives

_____
_____
_____
_____

Action Plan

_____
_____
_____
_____
_____

FOURTEEN
PRACTICE PERSISTENCE

Exercise

What two things did Grant learn at Vicksburg?

_____
_____
_____
_____
_____
_____
_____

How does innovation work?

_____
_____
_____
_____
_____
_____
_____

Name four mindsets to consider when attacking an obstacle.

_____
_____
_____
_____
_____
_____
_____
_____
_____

What is the phrase favored by Epictetus?

_____
_____
_____
_____
_____
_____
_____
_____

Personal Reflection

_____
_____
_____
_____
_____
_____
_____

Goals & Objectives

_____
_____
_____
_____

Action Plan

_____
_____
_____
_____
_____

FIFTEEN
ITERATE

Exercise

Under what conditions is failure seen as an asset?

_____
_____
_____
_____
_____
_____

What questions help birth alternative methods of execution?

_____
_____
_____
_____
_____
_____

Name four characteristics of entrepreneurs.

_____
_____
_____
_____
_____
_____
_____
_____

Which is one way we can guarantee not gaining from failure?

_____
_____
_____
_____
_____
_____
_____

Personal Reflection

_____
_____
_____
_____
_____
_____
_____

Goals & Objectives

_____
_____
_____
_____

Action Plan

_____
_____
_____
_____
_____

SIXTEEN
FOLLOW THE PROCESS

Exercise

What does Coach Nick Saban teach?

_____
_____
_____
_____
_____
_____
_____

What is the philosophy of the process?

_____
_____
_____
_____

How do you get out of being trapped?

_____
_____
_____
_____
_____
_____
_____
_____
_____

Name two things the process demands.

_____
_____
_____
_____
_____
_____
_____
_____
_____

Personal Reflection

_____
_____
_____
_____
_____
_____
_____

Goals & Objectives

_____
_____
_____
_____

Action Plan

_____
_____
_____
_____

SEVENTEEN
DO YOUR JOB, DO IT RIGHT

Exercise

Do you do your job right?

_____
_____
_____
_____
_____
_____

Would you say your job is an opportunity to learn and excel?

_____
_____
_____
_____
_____
_____

List three ethics with which you should respond, no matter what you face.

_____
_____
_____
_____
_____
_____
_____
_____

What is the answer to Viktor Frankl's question on the meaning of life?

_____
_____
_____
_____
_____
_____
_____

Personal Reflection

_____
_____
_____
_____
_____
_____
_____

Goals & Objectives

_____
_____
_____
_____

Action Plan

_____
_____
_____
_____

EIGHTEEN
WHAT'S RIGHT IS WHAT WORKS

Exercise

How did Samuel Zemurray solve the land conflict?

_____
_____
_____
_____
_____
_____

What is your mission and how far are you willing to go to reach it?

_____
_____
_____
_____
_____
_____

What is pragmatism?

_____
_____
_____
_____
_____
_____
_____
_____

Do you agree with the phrase – think progress, not perfection?

_____
_____
_____
_____
_____
_____
_____
_____

Personal Reflection

_____
_____
_____
_____
_____
_____
_____

Goals & Objectives

_____
_____
_____
_____

Action Plan

_____
_____
_____
_____
_____

NINETEEN
IN PRAISE OF THE FLANK ATTACK

Exercise

What was George Washington's war strategy?

_____
_____
_____
_____
_____
_____
_____

What do you understand by the line of least expectation?

_____
_____
_____
_____
_____
_____
_____

Give a reason why great masters seem to perform effortlessly.

_____
_____
_____
_____
_____
_____
_____
_____

Explain Kierkegaard's indirect communication.

_____
_____
_____
_____
_____
_____
_____
_____

Personal Reflection

_____
_____
_____
_____
_____
_____
_____
_____

Goals & Objectives

_____
_____
_____
_____

Action Plan

_____
_____
_____
_____
_____

TWENTY
USE OBSTACLES AGAINST THEMSELVES

Exercise

How did Gandhi use the British Empire against themselves?

_____
_____
_____
_____
_____
_____

What is the power of opposites?

_____
_____
_____
_____
_____

Recount an experience when you used restraint to oppose your obstacle.

_____
_____
_____
_____
_____
_____
_____
_____
_____

Has an obstacle ever made you explore a new direction?

_____
_____
_____
_____
_____
_____
_____
_____
_____

Personal Reflection

_____
_____
_____
_____
_____
_____

Goals & Objectives

_____
_____
_____
_____

Action Plan

_____
_____
_____
_____

TWENTY-ONE
CHANNEL YOUR ENERGY

Exercise

How did Arthur Ashe's emotional control and energy focus place him ahead of other tennis players?

_____
_____
_____
_____
_____
_____

Why was Louverture called the opening?

_____
_____
_____
_____
_____

What difficulty in your life could counter your channeling your energy?

_____
_____
_____
_____
_____
_____
_____

What are the advantages of being physically loose while maintaining mental restraint?

_____
_____
_____
_____
_____
_____
_____
_____
_____

Personal Reflection

_____
_____
_____
_____
_____
_____
_____
_____

Goals & Objectives

_____
_____
_____
_____

Action Plan

_____
_____
_____
_____
_____

TWENTY-TWO
SEIZE THE OFFENSIVE

Exercise

How did Barack Obama handle the race scandal in 2008?

_____
_____
_____
_____
_____
_____
_____

Do you agree with Obama's adviser Rahm Emmanuel concerning not letting a serious crisis go to waste?

_____
_____
_____
_____

How did Napoleon describe war?

_____
_____
_____
_____
_____
_____
_____
_____
_____

Have you had a teachable moment in the past? Describe it.

_____
_____
_____
_____
_____
_____
_____
_____
_____

Personal Reflection

_____
_____
_____
_____
_____
_____

Goals & Objectives

_____
_____
_____
_____

Action Plan

_____
_____
_____
_____
_____

TWENTY-THREE
PREPARE FOR NONE OF IT TO WORK

Exercise

Have you resolved not to stop trying, no matter what?

_____
_____
_____
_____
_____
_____

Do you believe that an obstacle sometimes might be an opportunity to practice other skills?

_____
_____
_____
_____

How does Duke Ellington define problems?

_____
_____
_____
_____
_____
_____
_____
_____

After trying tirelessly, will you accept the final verdict, whatever it is?

_____
_____
_____
_____
_____
_____
_____
_____

Personal Reflection

_____
_____
_____
_____
_____
_____
_____
_____

Goals & Objectives

_____
_____
_____
_____

Action Plan

_____
_____
_____
_____
_____

PART III

WILL

TWENTY-FOUR
THE DISCIPLINE OF THE WILL

Exercise

Do you believe that good things take time?

_____
_____
_____
_____
_____
_____
_____

List three functions of the will.

_____
_____
_____
_____
_____
_____

What builds your confidence?

_____
_____
_____
_____
_____
_____
_____
_____

What five lessons are the most critical to grappling difficulties?

_____
_____
_____
_____
_____
_____
_____
_____

Personal Reflection

_____
_____
_____
_____
_____
_____
_____

Goals & Objectives

_____
_____
_____
_____

Action Plan

_____
_____
_____
_____

TWENTY-FIVE
BUILD YOUR INNER CITADEL

<u>Exercise</u>

How did Theodore Roosevelt fight asthma?

_____
_____
_____
_____
_____
_____
_____
_____
_____

If things get worse, can you handle yourself?

_____
_____
_____

Does being alone scare you?

_____
_____
_____
_____
_____
_____
_____
_____
_____

Are you comfortable around uncertainty?

_____
_____
_____
_____
_____
_____
_____
_____
_____

Personal Reflection

_____
_____
_____
_____
_____
_____

Goals & Objectives

_____
_____
_____
_____

Action Plan

_____
_____
_____
_____

TWENTY-SIX ANTICIPATION
(THINKING NEGATIVELY)

Exercise

What is premortem?

_____
_____
_____
_____
_____
_____

When you set out to achieve a goal, do you always have a contingency plan?

_____
_____
_____
_____

What name did the stoics call premortem?

_____
_____
_____
_____
_____
_____
_____
_____

What maxim does common wisdom provide us with?

_____
_____
_____
_____
_____
_____
_____
_____
_____

Personal Reflection

_____
_____
_____
_____
_____
_____
_____

Goals & Objectives

_____
_____
_____
_____

Action Plan

_____
_____
_____
_____

TWENTY-SEVEN
THE ART OF ACQUIESCENCE

Exercise

What two options starred Thomas Jefferson in the face, and which did he chose?

_____
_____
_____
_____
_____
_____

What skills have you developed over time, as a result of constraints?

_____
_____
_____
_____
_____

What is the art of acquiescence?

_____
_____
_____
_____
_____
_____
_____
_____

Are you flexible enough to admit that there is always someone or something who could alter the plan?

_____
_____
_____
_____
_____
_____
_____
_____

Personal Reflection

_____
_____
_____
_____
_____
_____

Goals & Objectives

_____
_____
_____
_____

Action Plan

_____
_____
_____
_____

TWENTY-EIGHT
LOVE EVERYTHING THAT HAPPENS: AMOR FATI

Exercise

Has there been a time when you have endured tragedy and disappointment?

_____
_____
_____
_____
_____
_____

What is the next step after understanding that certain things are outside our control?

_____
_____
_____
_____
_____

Do you remain cheerful in all situations?

_____
_____
_____
_____
_____
_____
_____

Do you waste time looking back at your expectations?

_____
_____
_____
_____
_____
_____
_____
_____
_____

Personal Reflection

_____
_____
_____
_____
_____
_____
_____

Goals & Objectives

_____
_____
_____
_____

Action Plan

_____
_____
_____
_____
_____

TWENTY-NINE
PERSEVERANCE

Exercise

What is the difference between persistence and perseverance?

_____
_____
_____
_____
_____
_____
_____

What was the secret to Magellan's success?

_____
_____
_____
_____
_____

Do you agree that our actions can be constrained but our will can't be?

_____
_____
_____
_____
_____
_____
_____
_____
_____

What if the full meaning of KBO?

_____
_____
_____
_____
_____
_____
_____
_____

Personal Reflection

_____
_____
_____
_____
_____
_____
_____

Goals & Objectives

_____
_____
_____
_____

Action Plan

_____
_____
_____
_____
_____

THIRTY
SOMETHING BIGGER THAN YOURSELF

Exercise

What did Stockdale spend over seven years after his capture doing?

_____
_____
_____
_____
_____
_____

What was Stockdale's watchword?

_____
_____
_____
_____

Do you think of ways of solving problems so as to help others?

_____
_____
_____
_____
_____
_____
_____

How will you contribute to the betterment of the society?

_____
_____
_____
_____
_____
_____
_____
_____
_____

Personal Reflection

_____
_____
_____
_____
_____
_____
_____
_____

Goals & Objectives

_____
_____
_____
_____

Action Plan

_____
_____
_____
_____
_____

THIRTY-ONE
MEDITATE ON YOUR MORTALITY

Exercise

Recount a near-death experience, if you've ever had one.

_____
_____
_____
_____
_____
_____
_____
_____

What would you change about your life if you had limited time to live?

_____
_____
_____
_____

What part of the serenity prayer speaks most to you?

___

How do you come to terms with death?

___

Personal Reflection

_____
_____
_____
_____
_____
_____
_____

Goals & Objectives

_____
_____
_____
_____

Action Plan

_____
_____
_____
_____
_____

THIRTY-TWO
PREPARE TO START AGAIN

Exercise

How should you live life knowing there will always be obstacles?

_____
_____
_____
_____
_____
_____

Would you say that you have attended the best version of you?

_____
_____
_____
_____

Do you view life as a marathon or a sprint?

Does beating an obstacle help you build strength?

Personal Reflection

_____
_____
_____
_____
_____
_____
_____
_____

Goals & Objectives

_____
_____
_____
_____

Action Plan

_____
_____
_____
_____
_____

Made in United States
North Haven, CT
02 July 2025